The

WESTERN
GARDENER'S
JOURNAL

A Three-Year Almanac

D1469214

Text and Photography by Margaret Moulton

CHRONICLE BOOKS

Acknowledgments

Many thanks to all the gardeners who graciously welcomed me into their private domains. Endless gratitude to my editor, Leslie Jonath, for her confidence in me and in this project. Thanks to the readers who offered early criticism and encouragement — Suzanne Caporael, Donna Jaffe, Lianne Morrison, Jeanne Moulton, and John Rusmore. Most of all, thank you to my husband Rob Shaeffer for his constant support.

Printed in Hong Kong

10 9 8 7 6 5 4 3 2 1

ISBN 0-8118-1876-4

Photographs by Margaret Moulton

Illustrations by Anne Field

Distributed in Canada
by Raincoast Books
8680 Cambie Street
Vancouver, B.C. V6P 6M9

CHRONICLE BOOKS
85 Second Street
San Francisco, CA 94105
www.chronbooks.com

Art Direction and Design: Miranda Design, San Francisco

Dedicated

to my parents, Molly and Bob, who inspired me through their own delight in gardening, and to my daughters Brent and Faith, in hopes that they will grow up in a peaceful garden.

Table of Contents

INTRODUCTION

The pleasures of the western gardener are legion. Many plants bloom in winter, and many vegetables grow year-round. Unless we live in the harshest mountain climates, we can putter outside almost everyday of the year without suiting up against frostbite. Whether we garden in a balmy climate, coastal fog, mountain altitudes, or arid desert, we can take great pleasure in recording successes and disappointments, sketch out our dream gardens, or make notes for future use and possibly even for posterity.

Although I am not an organized gardener, one disciplined endeavor is to keep notes on everything I do together in one place. My garden records have always been written in a pretty little horticultural notebook intended for an English gardener. From month to month and year to year, I look up what I did previously and when I did it, how a plant grew and when it bloomed. I've often wished I could jot down my thoughts and record my experiences next to a picture of a plant that would thrive in my garden, with a timetable oriented toward the western climate. I wanted to be inspired by photographs of western natives, perennials with winter color, and winter-blooming annuals, or to study lists of suggested plants for a drought-tolerant garden. So I created the *Western Gardener's Journal*.

While researching the information in this book, I learned eye-opening facts about how backyard gardening affects the general biodiversity of our planet. I increasingly give consideration to what impact my gardening practices have on the ecology of my neighborhood, and I adopt habits and approaches that will help the overall ecological balance. I learned that one reason to plant natives and drought-tolerant plants in western gardens is that plants like peonies require too much water, too much synthetic fertilizer, too much coddling to produce only a few lush flowers. Natives, on the other hand, are naturally adapted to our specific climate zones and do not require anything extra but a little overdue appreciation.

Each month offers lists of planning, planting, and maintenance suggestions and brief essays on particular topics appropriate to the season. The Resources at the back of the journal include books of interest to the western gardener, sources for seeds and plants, and grid paper for you to plan or diagram you garden. These features, along with the photographs of western gardens, will hopefully inspire you to enjoy and record your garden observations and experiences the year round.

W I N T E R

How I Garden

I think about gardening as chefs approach creating a meal—imagining how the food will taste, how it will smell, how it will look, savoring the blend of flavors before the first garlic clove is peeled. They might make adjustments to a recipe or comments in the cookbook's margins, or note successful menu combinations. Similarly, when I think about garden planning, I imagine how I want the space to look and feel in its days of glorious bloom as well as in its times of quiet color. January offers the western gardener a chance to reflect on the possibilities of spring and summer while enjoying the harvest of a winter vegetable garden or the delight of birdsong from bushes laden with winter berries.

Drawing on my background as an artist and photographer, I watch how the light moves over my yard throughout the day and during the year. I imagine what the garden needs in terms of structure, texture, and color. Does the garden have enough light? Will a particular plant require too much extra water, and will it add to the visual mix without overpowering other plants? Should a plant stand as a central figure, like the main ingredient in a recipe; is it textural support, like potatoes in soup; or, is it a flash of color, like a pinch of cayenne? Rainy days are peaceful times to review notes from last year's garden—which plants suffered from disease or mildew, which tomatoes tasted the best, or how successful the seeds were started last spring. It is even useful to compare weather notes from the last few winters to see what rainfall and frost I might expect, and how soon I can start those seeds I'm about to order.

In these early stages of garden planning, you can benefit from making a rough garden map. Looking through magazines and catalogues, wandering through nurseries imagining various plants in your own garden, and noticing what works well or looks striking in other yards all help to get the creative juices flowing. But, just as in cooking, following a recipe exactly can limit your adventurous spirit, and a strict garden plan can frustrate the experimental gardener in all of us. I often sketch in some central figures that will be mainstays (rhododendrons, fruit trees, roses, native shrubs), then add other plants that would be fun to try in the garden. If a plant does well, I may add more to create a drift or spread a few throughout the garden for a repetitive accent. If something does not work in one place, I yank it, perhaps for transplant, perhaps for the compost pile.

This is not the approach of a professional landscape designer, who installs an entire garden at once. Money and time often limit the enthusiastic gardener's ability to plant everything simultaneously. But with a gradual approach, a garden is never finished. Puttering around, cutting back here, transplanting there, finding space for a beautiful new plant you could not resist at the nursery—these are the joys of gardening. They are also what is so great about living in the West. Certainly we prune at specific times and plant at others, but western gardeners can be in the garden twelve months of the year and enjoy any number of plants in their prime season of display or productivity.

Planning:

____ Order seeds for summer-blooming flowers and vegetables.

____ Sketch layout for summer vegetable garden.

____ Plan for crop rotation.

____ Design drip system while skeleton of garden is clearly visible.

Planting:

____ Plant bare-root plants (roses, fruit trees, cane berries).

____ Plant cover crop in vegetable beds.

____ Plant annuals for spring color in warm zones.

____ Sow seeds for lettuce.

____ Start seeds indoors or in cold frame for warm-season annuals and
vegetables in warm climates.

Maintenance:

____ Protect plants from frost if necessary on a daily basis: cover plants at
night and remove cover during daytime.

____ Prune dormant deciduous plants (roses, fruit and nut trees, grapes,
flowering vines).

____ Fertilize annuals, citrus, and cool-season lawns.

____ Spray dormant oils again against fungus on fruit, roses, nuts.

____ Clean, sharpen, and oil tools.

____ Control slugs and snails for smaller populations in summer.

____ Mulch and weed flower and vegetable beds.

____ Water if rain has been less than normal for season.

Year-round Lettuce

Lettuce can pose serious frustrations for any gardener, but if western gardeners are creative with locations and varieties, most areas can grow lettuce year-round, even in the mountain states and frost-prone areas. Because most lettuces do not like too much sun exposure, winter is a safe time to start seeds or plants in almost any part of your garden, even the sunniest areas. You can pick a very small plot and, after working plenty of compost into the soil, broadcast lettuce seeds or plant six-packs from the nursery. If cold temperatures threaten, you can build a simple cold frame that will shelter the seedlings and tender young plants.

Mesclun, a mixture of lettuce varieties and sometimes other greens, offer a good option in winter or summer because the plants need to grow only a few inches before you snip them with scissors for use in a flavorful salad mix. Sow the Mesclun seeds broadcast style, not in rows. Try to use a weed-free compost mix if you can, as it is sometimes difficult to differentiate the young weeds from the sprouted lettuce. To enjoy an ongoing crop, sow the seeds in successive time frames, maybe two weeks apart, so as one batch is used up, another is ready for harvest. You can also sow the lettuce in wide, shallow pots that can be protected from the cold or even placed in a kitchen greenhouse window.

Weed free compost mix
Plant 2 wks apart

dint
Lettuce

WEEK 1   year_____

Weather

When should I plant

Bloom/Harvest/Planting

Melon

Radish

Cantalope

Squash

Cucumber

OKRA

Maintenance

Planning

year_____   year_____

Weather   Weather

companion

Bloom/Harvest/Planting   Bloom/Harvest/Planting

Maintenance   Maintenance

Planning   Planning

JANUARY

Weather

Bloom/Harvest/Planting

Maintenance

Planning

year_____

year_____

Weather

Weather

Bloom/Harvest/Planting

Bloom/Harvest/Planting

Maintenance

Maintenance

Planning

Planning

JANUARY

Weather

Bloom/Harvest/Planting

Maintenance

Planning

year_____   year_____

Weather   Weather

Bloom/Harvest/Planting   Bloom/Harvest/Planting

Maintenance   Maintenance

Planning   Planning

JANUARY

WEEK 4   year_____

Weather

Bloom/Harvest/Planting

Maintenance

Planning

year_____   year_____

Weather

Weather

Bloom/Harvest/Planting

Bloom/Harvest/Planting

Maintenance

Maintenance

Planning

Planning

Horticultural Heirlooms

Heirloom seeds are just as valuable as heirloom linen and silver. The passing down of these treasures is worldwide, across backyard fences and through the generations. In the case of seeds, the objects hold within them the future as well as the past. Better still, heirloom seeds represent the diversity of climates on the planet; the parent plants have adapted to the vicissitudes of their particular region, making them even more valuable to local gardeners. In the West, February is a good time to prepare for seed starting, and though you won't save seeds from your own harvest until fall, you can use this month for researching and ordering heirlooms unique to your region, and experimenting with them when you start your own tried-and-true favorites.

Heirlooms are somewhat loosely defined as those plants that have been grown for more than one hundred years and can be propagated from year to year by seed, cutting, or division. Many heirloom plants carry with them a cultural as well as a biological heritage. For instance, in the West, you can still grow dry bush beans descended from ancient Anasazi culture in Mesa Verde. You can also grow runner beans that originated in the 1700s in Germany. Immigrants to the United States brought seeds from their homeland, saved the seeds of those plants that adapted well to the variations in western climate, and grew them year after year. These heirlooms were special in other ways, too. Not only did a certain tomato grow lustily in the Northwest, but its flavor was sweet and its flesh juicy. Or maybe a particular peach produced well in warm western regions with short chill periods. These plants are treasures whose value is without a price tag in the home gardeners' world.

For a commercial breeder, however, non-hybridized plants may have presented problems. The tomato's skin was too fragile for shipping or the peach did not ripen well off the tree, making these fruits unsuitable for commercial purposes. Ornamental plants such as old roses treasured for their heady fragrance might have been subject to disease in many climates and thus not practical for mass marketing. Unfortunately, commercial factors like these have severely limited our selection of produce in grocery stores and even our plant choices in many nurseries.

Although hybridized plants are bred to tolerate difficult growing conditions such as drought, pests, or vulnerability to virus, and they may offer early harvest and high yield, they are often dependent on chemical fertilizers or toxic pest controls to fulfill their promise. Also, the seeds of hybridized plants cannot be saved for next year's planting because they tend to revert to one parent strain or another or are completely sterile after the first harvest, making the gardener or farmer dependent on buying new seeds every year. This makes for good marketing, but not so sound gardening. Heirloom seeds, by contrast, are open pollinated, and therefore can reliably reproduce true to the parent plant. Home gardeners who save and sow their heirloom vegetable and flower seeds year after year contribute to the preservation of genetic diversity in our botanical population.

Planning:

_____ Plan for and buy summer-blooming bulbs.

Planting:

_____ Start warm-weather vegetable and flower seedlings indoors or in greenhouse or cold frame.

_____ Harden off, then plant lettuce seedlings outdoors if danger of frost past.

_____ Plant cool-weather vegetables outdoors (artichokes, broccoli, cabbage, cauliflower).

_____ Sow seeds for cool season vegetables outside (beets, carrots, chard, lettuce, peas, and spinach).

_____ Plant spring-blooming perennials.

_____ Plant summer-blooming bulbs (crocosmia, dahlias, tuberoses).

_____ Plant bare-root roses if not done earlier.

Maintenance:

_____ Protect plants from frost if necessary.

_____ Spray dormant oils again for fungus on roses, nut, and fruit trees.

_____ Clean, sharpen, and oil tools if not done in January.

_____ Test old seeds for germination viability.

_____ Fertilize fall planted annuals, perennials, and established trees and shrubs.

_____ Fertilize cool-season lawns if not done in January.

_____ Prepare soil for spring planting: work 2-6 inches of compost into soil throughout garden.

_____ Groom garden: hoe small weeds and pick up fallen blossoms.

_____ Continue to control slugs and snails.

_____ Water plants deeply if soil is dry from limited rain.

Testing Seeds for Viability

Just because you never planted that packet of lettuce seeds dated last year doesn't mean that the seeds must be tossed in the trash or compost. To test your leftover seeds, put five or ten seeds on a damp paper towel, and cover it with plastic or another paper towel to keep it moist. When the seeds have sprouted, figure out what percentage were successful and adjust accordingly when you sow. If five out of ten sprout, you'll have a 50 percent success rate. If the package instructions tell you to sow five seeds in an inch, double the amount to ten.

Bush Beans

'*Anasazi*': Reputed to have originated with the ancient Anasazi civilization near Mesa Verde. Heirloom; endangered.

'Boy': Bears person-shaped marking on beans. Drought resistant. Heirloom; endangered.

'Garbanzo': Native to India. Good for use in short-season dry areas, not foggy coastal areas.

'Montezuma's Red': California heirloom; endangered.

'Swedish Brown': High yield. Does well in coastal areas.

'Yellow Eye': Originated in eastern Washington. Drought resistant.

Pole Beans

'Fortex': Early, productive, 10-inch stringless French bean.

'Hopi Black': Prolific yield of tasty beans snap or dry. Endangered.

'Oregon Giant': Extra long pods. Does well in Northwest. Endangered.

Tomatoes

'Amish Paste': Good for sauces as well as fresh off vine.

'Bonny Best': Large red, round fruits good for home canning. Performs well in coastal areas. Heirloom.

'Green Zebra': Small striped fruit; green when ripe. Heirloom.

'Marvel Stripe': Striped red and orange fruit with intensely rich flavor. Needs long growing season.

Lettuces

'Bronce Rodon': Loose-leaf, green with red-trimmed edges.

'Brune d'Hiver': One hundred-year-old French variety, with long bronze leaves shaped like romaine, but with texture of 'Bibb.'

FEBRUARY

WEEK 1   year_____

Weather

Bloom/Harvest/Planting

Maintenance

Planning

year_____   year_____

Weather   Weather

Bloom/Harvest/Planting   Bloom/Harvest/Planting

Maintenance   Maintenance

Planning   Planning

FEBRUARY

Weather

Bloom/Harvest/Planting

Maintenance

Planning

year_____   year_____

Weather   Weather

Bloom/Harvest/Planting   Bloom/Harvest/Planting

Maintenance   Maintenance

Planning   Planning

FEBRUARY

WEEK 3   year_____

Weather

Bloom/Harvest/Planting

Maintenance

Planning

year_____   year_____

Weather

Weather

Bloom/Harvest/Planting

Bloom/Harvest/Planting

Maintenance

Maintenance

Planning

Planning

FEBRUARY

WEEK 4   year_____

Weather

Bloom/Harvest/Planting

Maintenance

Planning

year_____   year_____

Weather   Weather

Bloom/Harvest/Planting   Bloom/Harvest/Planting

Maintenance   Maintenance

Planning   Planning

Dreams of the Vegetable Gardener

For the western gardener, March poses as many frustrations as joys. There are breathtaking plants in bloom—Ceanothus, fruit trees, and native currants—but just as many perennials and trees still lie dormant, waiting for longer days and warmer nights before unfurling their spring wardrobes. In most regions, the sunny skies assure us that spring is near, and everyone is more than ready for it. But just as March weather graces us with some blissfully warm days and we get used to the warmth, it can surprise us with fierce winds and cold rain reminding us that it is not quite time to plant those warm weather vegetable starts from the greenhouse or nursery.

Around this time every year, we western gardeners start salivating at the thought of all the delicious vegetables and fruits that our gardens will grow. I always imagine the bountiful array of tomatoes, peppers, chiles, eggplants, cucumbers, apples—maybe even corn—that will spring from the fertile soil of my backyard. I even imagine enlarging my vegetable plot to accommodate these quantities. Then I remember reality: in my particular garden and microclimate, there aren't many hours of direct sun, and the summer fog often rolls in at the end of the day, causing dewy, damp nights, and disappears only by late morning the following day. The harsh reality in my garden is that space limits me to a few varieties and to those that thrive in this climate. On the brighter side, there are many plants that have proven to do well in this coastal climate, and with a long western growing season, I don't have to forget all my dreams of a bountiful harvest.

While many western gardeners cannot grow the range of chiles that thrive in hot gardens in the southwest, several varieties of tomatoes and sweet peppers do quite well throughout the West. Similarly, although some varieties of apples and peaches require a longer, deeper chill factor than a western garden can provide, many varieties produce very well in the warmer climates of the West.

Remembering these practical caveats, we can tame our wild imaginary gardens into reality and get to work planning rewarding gardens appropriate to our individual climate zones, holding our breath for another week or two until spring hits in full glory.

Planning:

_____ Plan new or revitalized herb garden; order seeds.

Planting:

_____ Plant summer annuals as weather warms toward end of month.

_____ Plant hardy landscape shrubs, woody perennials, and ground covers.

_____ Sow seeds for summer annuals.

_____ Rejuvenate older herbs, plant new herbs.

_____ Divide perennials and replant (except in coldest mountain regions).

Maintenance:

_____ Prune ornamental fruit and shrubs after flowering.

_____ Amend soil with compost to improve texture and water retention.

_____ Build compost pile in preparation for summer needs.

_____ Fertilize lawns, if not fed in February.

_____ Fertilize citrus, bedding plants, shrubs, trees, vines, and berry plants.

_____ Control weeds with mulching and hoeing.

_____ Prune out and cart away dead wood on shrubs and trees for fire safety.

_____ Control aphids and depopulate snails.

_____ Water if rain has been lighter than normal.

_____ Test irrigation lines for leaks and breaks; improve coverage where needed.

year_____

year_____

Weather

Weather

Bloom/Harvest/Planting

Bloom/Harvest/Planting

Maintenance

Maintenance

Planning

Planning

MARCH

Weather

Bloom/Harvest/Planting

Maintenance

Planning

year_____   year_____

Weather   Weather

Bloom/Harvest/Planting   Bloom/Harvest/Planting

Maintenance   Maintenance

Planning   Planning

MARCH   WEEK 4   year_____

Weather

Bloom/Harvest/Planting

Maintenance

Planning

year_____   year_____

Weather   Weather

Bloom/Harvest/Planting   Bloom/Harvest/Planting

Maintenance   Maintenance

Planning   Planning

WINTER

year_____

year_____   year_____

Summary   Summary   Summary

SPRING

The Aromas of Gardening

Gardening is often extolled for its therapeutic values— watering is meditative, digging builds muscles, and fresh air makes you feel alive. But one of the greatest treats in gardening is the unexpected smells. Sure, you expect flowers to entice you with their fragrance, but a handful of rich damp earth swells with potential—its aroma is unparalleled for inspiring gardening dreams. Digging in the garden becomes a sensory experience when the fresh smell of soil invades your being. You experience it as a tactile sensation, one of both memory and anticipation. It is not simply something you smell; it is something you taste and feel. (A fortune awaits the person who introduces a "soil" cologne.)

In the West we have so many plants whose smells are not just sweet, but spicy—earthy, actually. Their aromas can transport you. Brush up against a native currant plant *(Ribes sanguineum)* and the smell takes you to a peaceful walk in the redwoods—cool, damp, and quiet. The hot, fresh smell of a sage carries you to a dry trail climbing through chaparral. One moment you stand amid your backyard yarrows; the next you imagine yourself hiking in the mountains or walking along a coastal bluff. While you pull the weeds and trim back the oregano, you can dream about Italian villas; shape the lavender and imagine rustic picnics in Provence; water thyme and tarragon and absorb culinary inspiration. It is the magic of gardening that a plant's fragrance can envelop your whole being, drawing you into the garden and away from the worries of the world. Maybe we gardeners should introduce a new form of entertainment. Invite friends over to trim the herbs, dig in the compost, and thereby absorb the wonder of life through the smells of good, clean dirt.

Planning:

——— Double-check crop rotation plan before planting vegetables.

——— Shop for winter-tender plants, establish now in pots.

Planting:

——— Plant summer-blooming annuals and bulbs.

——— Harden off vegetable seedlings in cold-winter areas.

——— Plant dahlia bulbs in cold-winter areas.

——— Plant vegetable seedlings in last half of month in mild-winter areas.

——— Plant citrus.

——— Re-pot container plants.

Maintenance:

——— Prune frost-damaged plants after spring growth appears.

——— Prune spring-flowering shrubs (rhododendrons, azaleas, camellias) after bloom.

——— Control pests such as aphids, slugs, and snails.

——— Control weeds.

——— Check for nutrient deficiency, such as lack of iron or nitrogen, and remedy.

——— Groom garden by raking dead leaves and debris.

——— Trim hedges to shape back vigorous spring growth.

——— Mulch throughout garden.

The Earthworm Farm

Earthworms are low-maintenance, high-productivity tenants. They offer a compact way to compost your kitchen garbage while simultaneously producing a highly intense fertilizer for your garden. Red earthworms in a 2-foot-square compost bin consume two pounds of kitchen waste each week—about the output of an average two-person household. Compared with the average garden soil, their castings, excrement, are five times richer in nitrogen, seven times richer in usable phosphorous, eleven times as high in available potassium, and two times as high in calcium. Best of all, earthworms are undemanding. You feed them your garbage a couple of times a week, throw in a little shredded newspaper, and after a few months, you harvest black gold.

Building a worm farm is easy and offers a great educational experience for kids of any age. They can help tear up newspaper for the bin, release the worms, and feed them apple skins, carrot peelings, and other "worm food."

To establish a worm farm, use a container that is 10-16 inches deep, fit it with a lid, and provide 1/4-inch ventilation holes in the sides. Tear newspaper (black and white only) into 1-inch strips and fill the container to brimming full, then spray the shredded paper with water, turning it until it is lightly wet, like a wrung-out sponge. Feed the worms about one quart of kitchen scraps. These include anything you would put into a compost pile. Do not use meat or fish scraps, dairy products, grease, or any kind of animal feces. Let the worms adjust for a couple of weeks, then feed them one quart of kitchen waste per two square feet of surface area. Keep your worm farm in a place where it will not freeze or overheat and is protected from direct sun and rain. If using a plastic bin, you may need to add more newspaper to absorb extra moisture; if using a wooden bin, you may need to moisten the bedding. Always cover the kitchen scraps with fresh newspaper to discourage flies and odors; add fresh newspaper every couple of months.

Harvest worm compost as often as every two to three months and as infrequently as once a year. One method is to move all the existing bedding, worms, and castings to one side of the container, add fresh bedding and food to the other side and let the worms migrate over, then harvest from the deserted side of the container. Or you can dump the entire contents of the container onto a tarp in the sun. The worms will head quickly "underground" into the bottom of the pile, and you can lift off the rest and then place the worms into their house with fresh bedding and food. Or you can just reach in and scoop out the compost, worms included, and incorporate it into your garden soil.

WEEK 1   year 2024

Weather

Bloom/Harvest/Planting

Maintenance

Planning

year_____   year_____

Weather   Weather

Bloom/Harvest/Planting   Bloom/Harvest/Planting

Maintenance   Maintenance

Planning   Planning

WEEK 2   year_____

Weather

Bloom/Harvest/Planting

Maintenance

Planning

year_____   year_____

Weather   Weather

Bloom/Harvest/Planting   Bloom/Harvest/Planting

Maintenance   Maintenance

Planning   Planning

WEEK 3   year_____

Weather

Bloom/Harvest/Planting

Maintenance

Planning

year_____   year_____

Weather

Weather

Bloom/Harvest/Planting

Bloom/Harvest/Planting

Maintenance

Maintenance

Planning

Planning

APRIL

WEEK 4   year_____

Weather

Bloom/Harvest/Planting

Maintenance

Planning

year_____   year_____

Weather

Weather

Bloom/Harvest/Planting

Bloom/Harvest/Planting

Maintenance

Maintenance

Planning

Planning

Companion Planting

Companion planting is the time-honored practice of planting in close proximity combinations of plants that benefit each other. While the effectiveness has not been scientifically proven, many gardeners, herbalists, and horticulturists do agree that plant interactions can have both positive and negative impacts in your garden. Some plants attract beneficial insects; others serve to repel harmful insects. Just as some vegetables or herbs work together in a recipe—the way basil enhances tomatoes, or oregano adds extra pungency to beans—it is easy to understand that, as neighbors in the garden, these plants could benefit each other's overall health and flavor. Similarly, mixing herbs into a flower garden benefits the garden as a whole. In the mild-winter areas of the West, many herbs grow year-round, infusing the soil with aromatic oils that can both attract insects to or deter them from your flowers and shrubs.

Most companion planting practices involve herbs, but other considerations should be addressed as well. For instance, it is wise to consider the growing demands of particular plants when planning your garden. Do not plant two heavy feeders together; they will compete for nutrients in the soil. Similarly, if you stagger the bloom cycles of immediate neighbors in a flower garden, they will not demand blossom-supporting moisture at the same time of the season. Planting corn, pole beans, and pumpkins together provides both structural and nutritional support. After the ears of corn are harvested, the stalks act as poles for bean runners, and the broad leaves of the pumpkin plants shade the soil against evaporation while the beans and pumpkins mature. After harvest, all three can be tilled into the soil, to decompose over the winter, adding back nutrients to the soil.

Not all plants are well-matched neighbors. Some plants release substances that are toxic to other plants and can inhibit their growth. Experimenting in your own garden will certainly reveal these mismatches over time, but a little research on the subject will help you avoid planting unfriendly neighbors.

MAY

Planning:

____ Visit demonstration gardens, note names of plants that might do
     well in your garden.

____ Plan watering schedule for hot summer months.

Planting:

____ Plant vegetable seedlings if not done in April.

____ Plant flowering perennials (lavender, coreopsis, echinacea, yarrow).

____ Plant landscape shrubs, trees, and vines.

____ Plant drought-tolerant fruits (figs, strawberries, persimmons).

Maintenance:

____ Tend tomatoes and peppers: maintain even soil moisture, support
     with cages or stakes, and shade against sunburn.

____ Manage pests.

____ Feed subtropical plants (hibiscus, citrus, gardenias).

____ Feed rhododendrons and azaleas after blooming cycle is complete.

____ Prune rhododendrons, azaleas, and lilacs after bloom.

____ Aerate lawns, if needed.

____ Pinch back annuals for bushier growth and more flowers.

____ Move tender container plants for protection from hot afternoon sun.

____ Groom bulbs once foliage turns yellow.

____ Thin fruit for better size and healthier trees.

____ Control weeds with hoeing and mulching.

____ Remove spent rose blooms to encourage second round of blooming.

____ Clip hedges to shape new spring growth.

____ Water as necessary.

Beneficial Companions

Basil: Improves growth and flavor of tomatoes and peppers. Repels flies, tomato hornworms, and mosquitoes.

Borage: Improves growth and flavor of tomatoes, strawberries, and beans, and helps deter tomato hornworms. Its own bright blue flowers are edible.

Carrots: Grow well with peas, leaf lettuce, onions, and radishes.

Catnip: Plant in borders. Deters flea beetles as well as fleas. Invites cats to lounge in your garden, so don't plant near a bird feeder or birdbath.

Chamomile: Good for cucumbers and onions.

Chives: Improve growth and flavor of carrots and tomatoes. Keep away from beans and peas.

Dill: Beneficial to cabbage, onions and lettuce. Do not plant near carrots or tomatoes.

Flax: Companion to carrots and potatoes. Helps deter Colorado potato beetle.

French tarragon, marigolds, marjoram, thyme, valerian: Deter pests and promote healthy plants with good flavor.

Garlic: Improves growth and health of roses and raspberries. Helps repel aphids.

Horseradish: Plant at corners of potato patch to deter potato bugs.

Marigold: Key player in the companion planted garden. Deters general garden pests, especially tomato hornworms.

Nasturtium: Companion to radishes, cucumbers, squash, and melons. Helps repels white flies.

Onions: Good around beets, cabbage, carrots, and tomatoes. Keep away from beans and peas.

Parsley: Plant among asparagus and tomatoes.

Rosemary and sage (*Salvia officinalis*): Plant with beans, cabbage, and carrots. Keep sage away from cucumbers and onions.

Rue: Companion to roses and raspberries. Deters ants around fruit trees. Keep away from basil, cabbage, and sage.

Sunflowers: Help cucumbers thrive. Keep away from potatoes.

Tansy: Plant near roses, raspberries and fruit trees. Deters flying insects, ants, and striped cucumber beetles.

Thyme: Improves growth and flavor of eggplant, potatoes, and tomatoes.

Wormwood (*Artemesia absinthium*): Helps deter slugs. Harmful to most vegetables, so keep clear of the vegetable plot.

Yarrow (*Achillea*): Good throughout the garden. Enhances essential oil production of many herbs.

MAY

Weather

Bloom/Harvest/Planting

Maintenance

Planning

year_____   year_____

Weather

Weather

Bloom / Harvest / Planting

Bloom / Harvest / Planting

Maintenance

Maintenance

Planning

Planning

MAY

Weather

Bloom/Harvest/Planting

Maintenance

Planning

year_____

year_____

Weather

Weather

Bloom/Harvest/Planting

Bloom/Harvest/Planting

Maintenance

Maintenance

Planning

Planning

MAY

WEEK 3   year＿＿＿＿＿＿

Weather

Bloom/Harvest/Planting

Maintenance

Planning

year_____   year_____

Weather   Weather

Bloom/Harvest/Planting   Bloom/Harvest/Planting

Maintenance   Maintenance

Planning   Planning

MAY

year_____

Weather

Bloom/Harvest/Planting

Maintenance

Planning

year_____   year_____

Weather

Weather

Bloom/Harvest/Planting

Bloom/Harvest/Planting

Maintenance

Maintenance

Planning

Planning

Gardening with Children

Gardening with children—isn't that an oxymoron? How can you reach that satisfying, meditative place with a child nipping at your heels and stomping on your double-dug beds? For most gardeners with kids, even the chores of turning the compost and mowing the lawn offer an opportunity to work undisturbed, so why would you want to encourage them to join you in your place of experimentation and retreat? Besides, how can children really stay focused long enough to develop an appreciation for the gardening experience we love so much?

I am still learning that they might not, but that is not the point. Gardening with children is a double-edged shovel: it means you will not have the same experience you would have if planting, weeding and watering for a few peaceful hours by yourself. With a child assisting you, you will not get as much done and you may not get to do what you want. But you will experience countless moments of surprise and joy at the things children discover in the garden. After all, wouldn't you rather have your kids outside playing in the mud than inside staring glassy-eyed at the television? In fact, most gardening parents and gardeners who hang around kids want to share their love of the earth and all it gives to them. So how do you share your garden without ruining your perennials?

Speaking as one who has not yet mastered the concept, I think the first rule is to relax. Relax about what children can and cannot do in the garden and about which areas of your garden you are willing to see trashed and which areas are firmly off-limits. Relax about how well you can expect children to perform any task or chore they might undertake. Most of all, relax about whether or not they are going to like gardening as much as you do. Expose them to enough garden thought and garden practice, and hopefully it will become second nature to them. It did for me.

Next, find something that children can succeed at without too much managing. Even a two-year-old can help water the garden. This also gives you an opportunity to talk about using water wisely, a very important lesson in the West. Consider giving children their own little plot—perhaps an area you can relinquish without too many qualms. There is nothing like being able to shovel and rake in your own garden. If your garden space is limited, fill a wine-barrel planter with good soil, and let children dig, plant, and water in their own container garden.

Plant sure bets—things that will grow successfully in your yard and produce flowers or food. Sunflowers, for example, are colorful and grow with little attention except staking. Cucumbers produce on an earlier growing calendar than tomatoes. Of course, there is nothing like a cherry tomato bush loaded down with little red orbs to entice children into the wonders of fresh vegetables.

Planning:

_____ Plan for perennials to be planted in early fall.

Planting:

_____ Plant warm-weather vegetables and summer annuals if not done
earlier.

Maintenance:

_____ Water as necessary (do not water established natives).

_____ Support vegetables (tomatoes, peppers, melons) with stakes or cages.

_____ Cover fruit crops with light netting or floating row covers.

_____ Feed roses after each bloom cycle.

_____ Deadhead summer annuals to encourage further blooming.

_____ Manage weeds.

_____ Clear away fire-hazardous debris.

_____ Amend soil with compost.

Plants for Children

If you have enough space and your child is old enough to appreciate the wait, you can plant a special tree to commemorate a special day—a birthday or the year you moved to a new house—or a living Christmas tree that doesn't end up on the curb after the start of the new year.

Successful Children's Vegetables:
'Royalty Purple Pod' Runner Beans: Easy to see for harvesting because of bright purple color.

'Early Wonder Tall Top' Beets: Rewarding due to its early harvest maturity.

'Kinko' Carrots: Early variety. Does well in shallow soil.

'Tom Thumb' Popcorn: Ears 3–4 inches long on dwarf stalks, 3 feet tall. Extra early maturity, even in cold climates.

Nasturtiums: Sure, fast-growing bet for germination and bloom. Edible flowers.

'Giant Russian Mammoth' Sunflowers: Huge 12-inch flower heads of edible seeds on stalks 9–12 feet tall. Attracts bees, birds, and butterflies.

Western Native Trees for a Garden:
Madrone *(Arbutus menziesii):* Native from British Columbia to southern California and some areas of the Sierra Nevada. With its year-round peeling maroon bark, pinkish blooms in spring, and clusters of red berries in the fall, this 20-100 foot tree can lend year-round interest to almost any Western garden. (A. 'Marina' is a non-native hybrid that whose smaller size—20 feet—provides a good substitute for the home garden.)

California buckeye *(Aesculus californica):* Native to dry slopes and canyons of coastal ranges and Sierra Nevada foothills. Requires sun and room to spread its arching branches. Provides interest year-round: buckeyes hang from bare branches in fall and winter, brilliant green leaves in early spring, and candelabralike blooms April through June.

Western redbuds *(Cercis occidentalis):* Native to Arizona, California, and Utah, especially foothills of the Sierra Nevada.

Blue palo verde *(Cercidium floridum or C. torreyanum):* Relatively fast growing native of south-western desert. Stunning yellow flowers in April reward all who see the tree, as well as the child who planted it.

Western Natives for Living Christmas Trees:
Silver or cascade fir *(Abies amabilis):* Native from southern Alaska south to the coast ranges of Washington and Oregon. Grows as tall as 20 to 50 feet in gardens.

White fir *(A. concolor):* Native to mountains of southern Oregon, California, and Rocky Mountains. Slow grower up to 30 feet in gardens.

WEEK 1   year_____

Weather

Bloom/Harvest/Planting

Maintenance

Planning

year_____

year_____

Weather

Weather

Bloom/Harvest/Planting

Bloom/Harvest/Planting

Maintenance

Maintenance

Planning

Planning

JUNE

Weather

Bloom/Harvest/Planting

Maintenance

Planning

year_____   year_____

Weather

Weather

Bloom/Harvest/Planting

Bloom/Harvest/Planting

Maintenance

Maintenance

Planning

Planning

JUNE

WEEK 3   year_____

Weather

Bloom/Harvest/Planting

Maintenance

Planning

year_____

year_____

Weather

Weather

Bloom/Harvest/Planting

Bloom/Harvest/Planting

Maintenance

Maintenance

Planning

Planning

JUNE

WEEK 4   year_____

Weather

Bloom/Harvest/Planting

Maintenance

Planning

year_____

year_____

Weather

Weather

Bloom/Harvest/Planting

Bloom/Harvest/Planting

Maintenance

Maintenance

Planning

Planning

year_____   year_____   year_____

Summary   Summary   Summary

SUMMER

Landscaping for Fire and Water

Water gives life to everything, and we in the West live with that reality whether we garden or not. But for a western gardener, water determines the success or failure of every project, even in the rain-soaked Northwest. As if the water-rationing concerns were not enough, the past decade has taught westerners from mountainous Colorado to urban California the importance of fire-scaping—landscaping to protect homes from wildfires. While conserving water usage in the home and garden, we also need to create a garden landscape that discourages the spread of fire. The goal for any garden—an inviting, beautiful space—is actually quite compatible with having a landscape that is both drought-tolerant and firesafe.

Plant selection is key. Native plants rate high on lists of drought-tolerant plants as they have adapted to a dry climate by developing the ability to store moisture in small leaves. These same natives play an important part in a fire-safe landscape too, as long as they are well-maintained so dead wood is trimmed out and homes are made accessible to firefighters.

Succulents are often cited as the camels of drought-tolerant planting, but they can be a misleading choice for a water-wise garden. A popular choice in temperate western climates, ice plant *(Lampranthus sp.)*, is colorful (some say garishly so) and spreads quickly to cover a large area as a low-growing ground cover. However, most species are not native, and some horticulturists consider it an unwanted invasive plant that must be watered at least weekly in dry seasons to maintain its high moisture content.

Although lawns offer a comfortable addition to a garden, many western gardeners have grown wary of the undue amount of precious water that expanses of lawn require. Several alternatives can satisfy both a drought-tolerant enthusiast and a fire-safe planner. Let a lawn act as a greenbelt for your home, keeping moisture close to the structure. You can also attain almost the same look and feel of a grass lawn with a native grass meadow, which needs far less irrigation. Low-growing varieties of many herbs, such as thyme, chamomile, and yarrow, are worth considering as fire-resistant lawn substitutes.

Whether your garden is close to your house or farther out into your property, plan it with drought-tolerant fire deterrence in mind. Plant a core group of drought-tolerant spreading shrubs as the backbone of your landscape, then intersperse them with colorful annuals and ground covers in years when moisture levels are high. In wetter years, all the plants will get the necessary water, but in years with water rationing, plants that don't need as much water will keep your basic landscaping alive, whereas moisture-demanding flowers and annuals will die back.

P l a n n i n g:

___ Plan and order perennials for fall planting.

___ Plan and order spring-blooming bulbs for fall planting.

P l a n t i n g:

___ Plant fall crops (squash, beets, broccoli).

___ Start perennials for fall planting.

___ Not too late to plant out six-packs of summer-blooming annuals for
    color.

M a i n t e n a n c e:

___ Manage garden pests like spider mites and tomato hornworms.

___ Water in early morning, according to plant needs.

___ Harvest vegetables and fruits.

___ Mulch vegetable and flower beds with compost.

___ Pinch back herbs and annuals for bushier growth.

___ Tend fruit trees: thin fruit and support heavy limbs.

___ Tend roses: feed and water.

___ Feed cymbidiums.

___ Prune cane berries and stake new canes.

___ Control weeds with hand-pulling, hoeing, or soil solarization.

Fire Prevention and Drought Management

Fire-Safe Checklist:

1. Clear potential fuel sources—debris and dead wood among shrubs and trees, brush piles, combustible fuels—to 10 feet away from structures.

2. Prune out ladder fuels—branches and undergrowth that allow fire to travel up or down tree trunks.

3. Prune tree branches at least 15 feet away from chimney or stove pipes; cap all chimneys and stove pipes with wire mesh screening to prevent sparks from escaping.

4. Stack firewood at least 30 feet from your home or other structures; do not store beneath a wooden deck or stairway.

5. Consider installing a greenbelt of lawn or herbaceous plantings around your house.

6. Keep in mind when planting or thinning trees that there should be 10 feet between the edge of the canopies on level ground and 20 feet between canopies on a slope. Fire travels much faster uphill.

7. Make sure your home is easily accessible and defensible for firefighters: clearly mark your address, keep your driveway clear of overgrown vegetation, and ascertain that your house can be defended from any angle.

Drought-Tolerant Gardening Tactics:

1. Consider planting native plants appropriate for the precipitation patterns in your region.

2. Install a drip irrigation system.

3. Limit the size of any lawn area; water it with a timer on your irrigation system to avoid overwatering.

4. Water in early morning to allow the moisture to reach plant roots instead of in the mid-day heat which promotes evaporation. Afternoon and evening watering do not allow plants to dry off from any overhead spray, often leading to mildew and other fungal problems.

5. Mulch around trees, flowers, and vegetable beds (but not natives that require an arid landscape).

JULY

Weather

Bloom/Harvest/Planting

Maintenance

Planning

year_____   year_____

Weather

Weather

Bloom/Harvest/Planting

Bloom/Harvest/Planting

Maintenance

Maintenance

Planning

Planning

JULY

Weather

Bloom/Harvest/Planting

Maintenance

Planning

year_____   year_____

Weather   Weather

Bloom/Harvest/Planting   Bloom/Harvest/Planting

Maintenance   Maintenance

Planning   Planning

JULY

WEEK 3   year_____

Weather

Bloom/Harvest/Planting

Maintenance

Planning

year_____   year_____

Weather   Weather

Bloom/Harvest/Planting   Bloom/Harvest/Planting

Maintenance   Maintenance

Planning   Planning

WEEK 4   year_____

Weather

Bloom/Harvest/Planting

Maintenance

Planning

Weather

Weather

Bloom/Harvest/Planting

Bloom/Harvest/Planting

Maintenance

Maintenance

Planning

Planning

Nontoxic Pest Control

Garden pests come in all shapes and sizes, as large as deer and as small as mites and microscopic fungi. Many gardeners become frustrated dealing with garden predators; huge industries thrive from this fact, readily supplying gardeners with effective but toxic methods of nuking the little buggers. I've always worried about pesticides, so I asked other gardeners what they do to get rid of snails, aphids, and other pests. Everyone has their own methods. One woman hand-picks the snails off her plants, puts them in a jar with water (after squashing them), shakes it, and pours the "juice" around her vulnerable young plants. She swears it acts as a warning to other snails.

I gave up synthetic pesticides like some people give up caffeine—cold turkey. I likened my garden to my own body. Spraying my roses with pesticide to kill aphids seemed as unnecessary as treating poison oak with chemotherapy. Instead, a horticultural oil or a stiff blast from the garden hose will deter the tiny pests. Whereas an application of pesticides may kill all the bugs, both helpful and harmful, the less toxic methods may require more applications, but don't cause side effects.

Most organic pest-control manuals separate controls into varying levels of attack. Cultural controls include preventative methods for overall garden health: healthy soil, disease-resistant strains, companion planting, and crop rotation. Physical controls entail handpicking pests off plants, removing diseased leaves and fruit from the plants and the surrounding area, installing nets against birds and other animals, and using copper strips to keep snails away.

Biological controls use living organisms like beneficial insects and bacterial insecticides to manage pests. One summer my eggplant leaves withered under a fine webbing of unknown origin. Upon close inspection I discovered minuscule, orange spider mites sucking my plants. I called a supplier that sent predator mites to me overnight. Within days, the spider mites disappeared, and the eggplants grew new foliage and produced gorgeous purple orbs.

Acute or chemical controls such as pesticide sprays, sulfur and copper compounds, and botanical compounds are not completely nontoxic and should be used as a last resort. Some of the preventative treatments such as horticultural oils and organic copper sprays create inhospitable environments for many fungi and diseases. Others, like neem sprays, are much more toxic and should be applied only to ornamental, not edible, plants.

Learning about the pests in your garden and the best ways to manage them takes time, but is well worth the investment. Controlling pests does not mean eradication, but toleration of a certain level of unwanted pests. After all, eradication upsets the natural population balance. We share our gardens with more than our human friends. There's a whole wild population out there that depends on the plants in our gardens for sustenance.

Planning:

_____ Order or purchase native irises at local nursery.

Planting:

_____ Sow seeds for fall annuals (calendula, stock, violas).

_____ Sow seeds for cool-season vegetables (beets, carrots, chard, lettuce, peas).

_____ Plant bearded and native irises, or divide existing plants six weeks after flowers have faded.

_____ Plant fall-blooming bulbs (species crocus, meadow saffron, spider lily).

_____ Sow seeds for early-blooming sweet peas in temperate zones.

_____ Sow seeds or plant out six-packs of sunflowers in warm regions, for one last blast of color in the fall.

Maintenance:

_____ Water in early morning, according to plant needs.

_____ Deeply water large trees and shrubs.

_____ Protect against brush fire.

_____ Harvest vegetables and fruits.

_____ Groom garden: pick up fallen fruits and vegetables, shape plants, and remove weeds.

_____ Deadhead flowers and fertilize to keep them blooming into the fall.

_____ Feed roses after each blooming cycle, and water in early morning as needed.

_____ Amend soil in beds for fall planting.

_____ Prune cane berries and stake new canes.

_____ Continue to add organic mulch to entire garden to improve soil composition and conserve soil moisture.

Alternative Pest Controls

These less toxic solutions to some garden pests help manage the pest populations in your garden—they do not eradicate them. Most require repeated treatments with ongoing attention to the problem.

Aphids:

1. Apply a forceful spray of water from a hose to knock them off plants. I always add a few verbal threats for good measure.

2. Spray with one of the commercial "safe" soap solutions.

3. Release ladybugs, as a natural predator of aphids, into your garden.

4. Plant nasturtiums as companions to help repel aphids around and amid the afflicted plants.

Snails and Slugs:

1. Handpick year-round from walls, fences—wherever you see them. This is best done in early morning, before snails and slugs go to their shady hiding places to escape the heat of the day.

2. Install protective barriers of metal, particularly copper, which repel snails and slugs. Bend the top 2 inches of the barrier away from bed or the plant border. Snails and slugs also avoid rough mulches of wood shavings or oak leaves.

3. Use a beer-bait trap, a wide, shallow bowl filled with stale beer and recessed into the ground. The smell of fermentation attracts snails, which dive in, never to climb out.

Tomato Hornworms:

1. The bright green, 2-inch-long, horned creatures virtually disappear amidst the foliage of a healthy tomato plant. Handpick by looking for the granular black droppings, then start searching the leaves above that area. Pluck off the worms and dispose of them away from your garden.

2. Spray with commercial Bacillus thuringiensis (BT), a biological control safe for humans and other plants.

Weeds:

1. Maintain a healthy lawn so weeds cannot gain a foothold. Water and fertilize with organic fertilizer on a regular schedule. Mow your lawn to keep it healthy and to keep any existing weeds in check.

2. Hand-pull and hoe weeds in and among vegetables and flowers. Eliminating them before they go to seed, thus limiting their spread is the best method of control.

AUGUST

Weather

Bloom/Harvest/Planting

Maintenance

Planning

year_____   year_____

Weather

Weather

Bloom/Harvest/Planting

Bloom/Harvest/Planting

Maintenance

Maintenance

Planning

Planning

AUGUST

Weather

Bloom/Harvest/Planting

Maintenance

Planning

Weather

Weather

Bloom/Harvest/Planting

Bloom/Harvest/Planting

Maintenance

Maintenance

Planning

Planning

AUGUST

Weather

Bloom/Harvest/Planting

Maintenance

Planning

year_____   year_____

Weather   Weather

Bloom/Harvest/Planting   Bloom/Harvest/Planting

Maintenance   Maintenance

Planning   Planning

AUGUST

WEEK 4   year_____

Weather

Bloom/Harvest/Planting

Maintenance

Planning

year_____   year_____

Weather   Weather

Bloom/Harvest/Planting   Bloom/Harvest/Planting

Maintenance   Maintenance

Planning   Planning

A Month of Change

September is a month of change in the western garden. The weather is still warm and summery, and it seems too early for fall, but no matter where you live in the West, gardens begin to look bedraggled and gray. While vegetable gardens are still in their harvest prime, much of the once-thick summer foliage looks thin and dry, and summer-flowering plants only put out a minimal blooming effort as they begin to conserve their energy for cool-weather survival. Instead of ruing the loss of summer color, celebrate that your garden holds a colorful winter in its future, something easterners will envy while they shiver under winter snows. Now is the time to plan for seasonal color to enliven your winter views.

If you live in warmer zones (southern California and desert areas), color can come from annuals including Iceland poppies and pansies. Warm-climate perennials that offer color in winter include salvias, Mexican marigolds, society garlic, agapanthus, day lilies, and camellias. Cooler, wetter climate zones like those of northern California look to the striking deciduous magnolia trees for exotic flowers in late January and February, as well as to climbing vines such as jasmine, potato vine, and evergreen clematis. Both areas can depend on aloes for bright spots of color throughout Western winter months.

Colorful barks offer unexpected beauty in a winter garden in cold-winter western climates like the Northwest and mountain states. Nothing catches my breath like coral bark maple (*Acer palmatum 'Sango Kaku'*), redtwig and yellowtwig dogwoods (many are Western natives), and green-barked *Kerria japonica*. They will stand out in your winter garden whether you live in the Northwest, the mountain states, or northern California. All in all, September is a month to revel in your harvests from the summer, and plan for fall and winter color in your garden.

SEPTEMBER

Planning:

_____ Buy spring-blooming bulbs for planting in late October or
November.

_____ Research dahlias during height of bloom cycle, and note favorite
varieties.

_____ Pre-chill spring-blooming bulbs

Planting:

_____ Plant perennials and natives.

_____ Plant fall-blooming bulbs.

_____ Plant cool-season annuals for bright color in colder months.

_____ Plant or sow seeds for cool-season vegetables.

Maintenance:

_____ Harvest vegetables and fruits.

_____ Feed established landscaping plants to help them recover from
summer heat.

_____ Water as necessary.

_____ Protect against brush fire.

_____ For fire safety, prune and cart away dead twigs and stems on shrubs
and trees.

_____ Re-seed lawns if necessary, and fertilize.

_____ Manage pests.

_____ Prepare beds for fall planting.

Plants for Winter Color

Harsh Mountain Climates

Winter honeysuckle *(Lonicera fragrantissima):* Fragrant white blooms in late winter to early spring. Deciduous, hardy to 10,000 feet elevation. Plant with summer-blooming vine to cover ungainly form in summer months

Redtwig and red-osier dogwood *(Cornus stolonifera or C. sericea)* and yellowtwig dogwood *(C.s.flaviramea):* Striking bark adds color and sculpural interest to the winter garden. Deciduous; hardy to 10,000 feet elevation.

Japanese barberry *(Berberis thunderbergii):* Thorny, magenta stems and bright red berries add both color and texture to winter gardens. Plant individually or as a hedge. Deciduous; hardy to -20 F.

Rosa rugosa: Abundance of orange and red, 1-inch hips or fruit stud branches throughout winter. Deciduous; very hardy to freezes, winds, dry climates, and salt spray in coastal areas.

Pacific Northwest

All of the above suggestions plus:

Flowering cabbage *(Brassicaceae):* Purple-foliage plants, 10 inches tall, add color if planted in groups or singly in the ground or in pots. Can withstand light frost.

Winter daphne *(Daphne odora):* Extremely fragrant pink clusters of blossoms adorn this shrub in late February through March.

Mild Coastal and Inland Climates

All of the above suggestions plus:

Saucer magnolia *(Magnolia Soulangiana):* Deciduous trees up to 25 feet tall bring mid-to-late winter drama with huge, saucer-shaped, violet-pink and white flowers, 4 to 6 inches across. Not good in high wind areas and subject to frost damage. Star magnolia *(M. Stellata)* is hardier than *M. Soulangiana*, and has smaller, more delicate white flowers.

Snapdragons *(Antirrhinum majus):* These tall annuals, up to 3 feet, can add a wide range of color to mild winter gardens.

Desert Climates

Some of the above suggestions (check for heat and drought tolerance) plus:

Western redbud *(Cercis occidentalis):* A harbinger of spring with deep pinkish red buds dotting narrow, arching branches. Western native; hardy to 4,000 feet.

Chocolate daisy *(Berlandiera lyrata):* Yellow-flowering shrub adds year-round drought tolerant color and an unmistakable chocolate fragrance to the garden.

SEPTEMBER

WEEK 1   year_____

Weather

Bloom/Harvest/Planting

Maintenance

Planning

year_____   year_____

Weather

Weather

Bloom/Harvest/Planting

Bloom/Harvest/Planting

Maintenance

Maintenance

Planning

Planning

WEEK 2   year_____

Weather

Bloom/Harvest/Planting

Maintenance

Planning

year_____   year_____

Weather   Weather

Bloom/Harvest/Planting   Bloom/Harvest/Planting

Maintenance   Maintenance

Planning   Planning

SEPTEMBER

WEEK 3   year_____

Weather

Bloom/Harvest/Planting

Maintenance

Planning

year_____   year_____

Weather   Weather

Bloom/Harvest/Planting   Bloom/Harvest/Planting

Maintenance   Maintenance

Planning   Planning

SEPTEMBER

WEEK 4   year_____

Weather

Bloom/Harvest/Planting

Maintenance

Planning

year_____

year_____

Weather

Weather

Bloom/Harvest/Planting

Bloom/Harvest/Planting

Maintenance

Maintenance

Planning

Planning

year_____

year_____

year_____

Summary

Summary

Summary

AUTUMN

Planting Natives

Why plant natives? Aren't they just rangy, dry-looking plants that never bloom? On the contrary, native plants offer obvious advantages to home gardeners. If you add native plants to your garden palette, they will require less water, and less (if any) fertilizing than exotics and will need minimal pruning. If you are careful to choose plants native to your area, they will be virtually disease-resistant, having made the necessary genetic adaptations thousands of years ago, and will not be prone to frost damage. Birds and butterflies native to your area will recognize their old friends and visit them in your garden, subsequently distributing the seeds, nectars, and pollens even farther afield.

October is prime time for planting natives. Although they will take root and grow year-round, fall's cooler temperatures and precipitation allow the plants to grow into their new home and become established before bloom time next spring. Natives can mix well with introduced species, adding unexpected structure and texture to the garden. Native buckwheats like *Eriogonum arborescens* bring delicate gray-green foliage color, with wide, flat mauve blooms in summer. In shades ranging from white through blues to deep purple, wild lilacs *(Ceanothus)* offer a stunning native alternative to the traditional lilac. Their heart-stopping blue flowers can cover a hillside, grow into sculptural shrubs, or provide dense ground cover year-round in all Western regions. (Most varieties suffer from root rot if given too much water without good drainage. Keep away from direct water sources or plant on a hillside for good drainage.)

Native plants are enjoying a renaissance of appreciation from scientists and gardeners alike. Many native plants around the world are endangered—choked off by exotics that adapted well to new growing conditions—but suppliers and gardeners are reintroducing languishing species back into the gardener's repertoire. It is important that you check with your local agricultural extension before introducing a new species to your area. One region's glorious flower is sometimes another's uncontrollable weed.

OCTOBER

Planning:

_____ Order bare-root fruit trees, berries, and grapes.

_____ Order spring-blooming bulbs if not done earlier.

Planting:

_____ Plant perennials, shrubs, and ground covers to take advantage of winter moisture.

_____ Plant cool-season annuals (calendulas, nemesias, snapdragons, Iceland poppies).

_____ Plant bulbs in containers and in garden; pre-chill tulip and hyacinth bulbs.

_____ Set out garlic and onions.

_____ Sow wildflower seeds for spring bloom.

Maintenance:

_____ Thin cool-season vegetable seedlings.

_____ Cut back established perennials to within a few inches of the ground.

_____ Divide perennials if necessary, re-plant or share with friends.

_____ Groom garden: pick up dead leaves, weed, remove debris, and deadhead blooming annuals.

_____ Wait to prune until deep into dormant season or in late spring.

_____ Manage garden pests.

_____ Amend soil with compost.

_____ Fertilize lawn if not done in recent months.

_____ Water as necessary.

Western Native Plants for Color

Bearberry *(Arctostaphylos uva-ursi):* Evergreen ground cover with delicate white flowers in spring, red berries summer through fall.

Buckwheat *(Eriogonum):* Many varieties of this perennial, with varying heights and growth habits. Santa Cruz Island buckwheat *(E. arborescens)* grows about 4 feet high and has grayish-green foliage and rosy pink flat-headed clusters of dry-looking flowers. Blooms early summer into fall. Striking planted en masse.

Coral Bells *(Heuchera sanguinea):* Clumping perennial with 2 foot spikes topped with tiny bell-shaped flowers, colored white to deep coral, depending on variety. Blooms almost year-round in milder climates. Western columbine *(Aquilegia formosa):* Perennial with delicate, semi-deciduous foliage and yellow or red butterfly-shaped flowers.

Flowering currant *(Ribes sanguineum):* Deciduous, 4 to 12 feet tall, open-growth shrub whose pendulous groups of delicate, dark pink flowers in early spring can provide a lovely backdrop or striking group planting. Light green maple like foliage has spicy smell of rich, damp soil.

Flannel Bush *(Fremontia californicum):* Evergreen shrub 6 to 20 feet tall with 1 1/2-inch golden yellow flowers.

Breathtaking during bloom cycle in May and June.

Wild lilac *(Ceanothus):* Many varieties with growth habits from ground covers to small trees. Clusters of blue, white, and lavender flowers bloom February through April, depending on climate zone and species.

Manzanita *(Arctostaphylos):* The color provided by this sculptural native comes from its magenta bark, but it also blooms in spring with tiny bell-shaped flowers drooping among the spare, gray-green foliage. Ranging from ground cover to small trees, this western native requires little water once established.

Spice Bush *(Calycanthus occidentalis):* Perennial deciduous shrub, 4 to 12 feet tall, whose reddish-brown flowers add fragrance and add mystery to the back of borders. Blooms mid-spring through summer. Evergreen. Mostly native to California; some species grow in the Northwest, Rocky Mountains, and Southwest.

Yarrow *(Achillea millefolium):* Perennial, var. lauosa or 'Mountain' yarrow has gray-green foliage on 3 foot stems and sports lacy white caps that bloom late spring through early fall. Var. 'Rosea' or 'Cerise Queen' grow 2 to 3 feet tall with flat clusters of rosy to dusty red blooms summer through mid fall.

OCTOBER

Weather

Bloom/Harvest/Planting

Maintenance

Planning

year_____

year_____

Weather

Weather

Bloom/Harvest/Planting

Bloom/Harvest/Planting

Maintenance

Maintenance

Planning

Planning

OCTOBER

Weather

Bloom/Harvest/Planting

Maintenance

Planning

year_____   year_____

Weather   Weather

Bloom/Harvest/Planting   Bloom/Harvest/Planting

Maintenance   Maintenance

Planning   Planning

OCTOBER

WEEK 3   year_____

Weather

Bloom/Harvest/Planting

Maintenance

Planning

year_____   year_____

Weather

Weather

Bloom/Harvest/Planting

Bloom/Harvest/Planting

Maintenance

Maintenance

Planning

Planning

WEEK 4   year_____

Weather

Bloom/Harvest/Planting

Maintenance

Planning

year_____ year_____

Weather

Weather

Bloom/Harvest/Planting

Bloom/Harvest/Planting

Maintenance

Maintenance

Planning

Planning

Western Soils

Building up soil is a combination of art and investment. It takes days—actually years—of back-breaking labor to get just the right color and texture, finally creating a fertile soil rich with potential. It is a never-ending chore: carry kitchen scraps out to the compost pile, turn them in, wait, add lawn and shrub cuttings, turn, wait, and, finally, dig the compost into the stubborn, heavy soil. What always amazes me is that it works. The soil in my garden, especially the vegetable beds which get extra attention, improves every year.

November is a good time for the western gardener to prepare for next spring's soil improvement. Heavy soils like those in the dry regions of the West are higher in alkalinity and contain small particles that compact readily. These clay soils make it difficult for water and air to penetrate, not to mention being difficult to dig. Roots have limited space to grow, and once the clay soil absorbs water, it drains very slowly, creating prime conditions for diseases like root rot. Soils in areas with high rainfall like western Washington, Oregon, and the north coast of California are more acidic, often with a sandier texture. They drain more quickly, but vital nutrients often wash out with the draining water. The ideal loamy soil takes many seasons of gardening to perfect, but various approaches can add to the mix. You can take all those fallen leaves and dead vegetable plants and mix them with kitchen scraps, grass clippings, and manure to build a compost pile that cooks slowly over the winter, ready for use when you need it in spring.

The back-breaking labor of amending soil is not a one time chore. Because organic components break down in the soil, you cannot permanently build the organic matter in your soil. It is this very process of decomposition that improves soil structure by adding crucial nutrients and introducing particles that will hold water and nutrients in sandy soil and break up clumps of clay soil, allowing for better aeration as well as good drainage. Maintain the integrity of your soil by continuing to amend it on a yearly, if not seasonal basis, by digging in more amendments every time you plant. This is especially important in gardens where you don't have the luxury of several acres, which would give you enough arable land to let some of it lie fallow for several seasons. By adding loads of compost every year, you can renew and refresh your tired soil.

Planning:

——— Buy bare-root plants.

——— Research seeds for summer-blooming vegetables and flowers.

Planting:

——— Plant native shrubs and perennials in warm western regions.

——— In containers, plant indoor-blooming bulbs like fragrant narcissus as holiday gifts.

——— Plant spring-blooming bulbs.

——— Plant winter and early-spring annuals.

——— Plant nitrogen-fixing cover crops in vegetable beds.

Maintenance:

——— Protect plants from frost if necessary.

——— Clean up garden: pull faded summer annuals, rake dead leaves, and cut back perennials.

——— Manage weeds.

——— Build compost pile with dead leaves and pruned branches (avoid diseased plants, rose bushes, or Bermuda grass).

——— Control garden pests.

——— Water as necessary.

Amending the Soil

Soil—its texture and structure—profoundly affects the success of your garden, as much or more than irrigation. Whatever amount of water you give your garden may make no difference if your soil's structure is too heavy (clay) or too light (sand). Soil that is well balanced in both texture and minerals serves several vital functions for plant growth. It acts as the mechanical support for plants and their root systems, it functions as a source and reservoir for water and nutrients crucial to plant growth, and it allows air to move freely around the roots, supplying them with oxygen and room to grow. The ideal soil, loam, forms a loose clump when squeezed in your hand, and it holds together until dropped,when it breaks apart easily. Loam is rich in organic matter and drains well, yet retains the appropriate amount of moisture for plants to absorb.

Three minerals—nitrogen, phosphate, and potassium—are crucial for various stages of plant development and are absorbed most readily through the roots in the soil. To manage the relative mineral balance of your soil, you can have it tested, then add the necessary nutrients via organic or inorganic methods. But far more important is the improvement of your soil's texture, achieved primarily through organic amendments.

The two most useful and simplest organic amendments are compost (homemade or commercial) and barnyard manure (especially chicken, the highest in necessary nutrients). These organic amendments provide most of the nutrients your plants need, and they do not require extra nitrogen for decomposition, as do other organic amendments like peat moss or sawdust.

Planting a cover crop in the fall, usually fava beans or clover, revitalizes your soil by soaking up nutrients in the air and water and fixing them in nodules on the roots. When spring comes, dig the green plants under four to six weeks before planting, and your plants will thank you for the nutrient-rich soil. Crop rotation also breaks the cycle of pests and diseases by disrupting the breeding and feeding cycles in their preferred environment. Tilling the soil crushes the pests, as well as exposing the insects and fungus to sun and air and drying them out.

NOVEMBER

WEEK 1   year_____

Weather

Bloom/Harvest/Planting

Maintenance

Planning

year_____   year_____

Weather

Weather

Bloom/Harvest/Planting

Bloom/Harvest/Planting

Maintenance

Maintenance

Planning

Planning

NOVEMBER

WEEK 2   year_____

Weather

Bloom/Harvest/Planting

Maintenance

Planning

year_____

year_____

Weather

Weather

Bloom/Harvest/Planting

Bloom/Harvest/Planting

Maintenance

Maintenance

Planning

Planning

NOVEMBER

WEEK 3   year_____

Weather

Bloom/Harvest/Planting

Maintenance

Planning

year_____   year_____

Weather

Weather

Bloom/Harvest/Planting

Bloom/Harvest/Planting

Maintenance

Maintenance

Planning

Planning

NOVEMBER

WEEK 4   year_____

Weather

Bloom/Harvest/Planting

Maintenance

Planning

year_____   year_____

Weather   Weather

Bloom/Harvest/Planting   Bloom/Harvest/Planting

Maintenance   Maintenance

Planning   Planning

Wintertime Pleasures and Chores

Even in the West, gardening in the winter requires more fortitude than gardening in the balmy autumn months or blissful days of early spring. I just relearned a lesson I should never have forgotten: living in the temperate-winter areas of the West can lull gardeners into laziness. (Except for those who live in more severe mountain climate zones where snow, hail, and high winds can quickly reduce a garden to compost-makings.) An unusually severe frost caught me by surprise. Some of the obviously tender plants survived because by starlight I brought in the cymbidiums and covered the chard and lettuce. I forgot that, hand in hand with the thrill of watching my breath form little white clouds in the cold air, I had to think like a farmer: read the weather reports, listen to the news, and prepare for weather that can harm the garden. Wherever you garden, winter is a time of watching and preparing, and all the related chores can not go undone.

But even with its satisfying jobs like cleaning and oiling tools, sorting out empty pots, and preparing the greenhouse or cold frames for seed starting, winter confronts me with a task I would just as soon ignore—pruning. It seems that the more I learn about this overwhelming subject, the more questions I have. Rose pruning in particular taunts my gardening confidence. I'm convinced that one wrong move and the thorns will scar for life, or worse yet, ruin the rose bush. Since our western climate doesn't get cold enough to require radical pruning and deep mulching, I'm never sure how much I should prune. No matter how many books I read or experts I consult, every time I face a rosebush at pruning time I am intimidated. But each year I overcome my fears and snip away with my shears, holding my breath and hoping I've correctly interpreted the directions. In fact, the plants don't die—they thrive. Either I am lucky or I am learning.

The barrenness of pruned branches allows us to see into the garden in ways we can't in the verdant seasons. Holes in the overall planting show themselves, and we can fill many hours pondering just the right plant to fill the gaps. A pleasant way to fill those empty garden spaces and busy idle hands also benefits wildlife in the garden. Plants like *Viburnum davidi*, with its bright turquoise winter berries, offer a colorful view for humans and nutrition for birds and squirrels. Another entertaining and helpful approach is one I always loved as a child—bird feeders. Feeders with sugar solution for hummingbirds or seeds for songbirds bring a different form of life and color to a winter garden.

Another option for garden entertainment during the winter lull is education. Learn more about gardening by reading books, researching plants and seeds in regional journals and almanacs, or taking workshops—maybe even a class about pruning! Perusing catalogues for the perfect weeding tool or garden shears can fill many free moments, just as a good book of garden lore can be the stuff of dreams. But perhaps the best non-working moment is still spent in your garden—breathing the air, watching the birds, and knowing that for you, in your western garden, spring is truly around the corner.

Planning:

___ Buy bare-root plants.

___ Research seed catalogues for summer-blooming vegetables and
flowers.

Planting:

___ Plant native shrubs and perennials, unless soil is soggy.

___ Start planting dormant-season bare-root plants (roses, fruit trees,
berries, grapes).

___ Plant spring-blooming bulbs if not already done.

Maintenance:

___ Spray dormant plants with dormant oil as soon as leaves drop.

___ Protect plants from frost if necessary.

___ Groom garden to keep it free of dead foliage and weeds.

___ Wash out pots; dry and store with good air circulation.

___ Water as necessary if rains have been meager.

Catering to Wildlife

While you dream about the garden that will bloom next spring and summer, consider inviting a few entertaining guests. Rose hips, persimmons, and berries not only add color to your landscape, but provide much-appreciated sustenance for local and migratory birds. In spring, hummingbirds and butterflies always add spice to a day in the garden, as well as pollinating your plants and trees. Hummingbirds like bright red flowers. Here are a few to consider:

'Sitka' columbine *(Aquilegia)*, rose mallow *(Hibiscus moscheutos)*, cosmos *(C. bipinnatus)*, 'Garnet' or 'Firecracker' Penstemmon *(P. gloxinioides or P. eatonii)*, and Shirley poppy *(Papever rhoeas)*. Butterflies head for *Buddleia davidii* (commonly known as 'butterfly bush'), 'Barberry' *(Berberis)*, 'Apache plume' *(Fallugia paradoxa)*, and 'St. John's Wort' *(Hypercium)*.

You don't want to forget to offer food for suburban wildlife. Plants that produce berries and nuts can feed the squirrels and still beautify your garden. Conifer cones provide seeds for animals and shade for humans, along with the calming sound of the wind rustling the uppermost branches. Remember that suburbia took away more than open range for deer. We humans can meet our thirst with a turn of the faucet, but the deer hiding in a suburban neighborhood have lost their free-flowing sources. If you're not opposed to deer in your yard, consider setting out a few wide, low platters, attached to your drip system for the deer to slake their thirst as needed.

While it is important to protect your hard-won harvest from wild neighbors, it is also rewarding to devise methods of protection that allow everyone to share the bounty of your garden. The birds can still eat berries on *Viburnums (V. davidii)* while you protect your raspberries and stone fruits with lightweight netting.

DECEMBER

WEEK 1   year_____

Weather

Bloom/Harvest/Planting

Maintenance

Planning

year_____   year_____

Weather

Weather

Bloom / Harvest / Planting

Bloom / Harvest / Planting

Maintenance

Maintenance

Planning

Planning

DECEMBER

WEEK 2   year_____

Weather

Bloom/Harvest/Planting

Maintenance

Planning

year_____   year_____

Weather   Weather

Bloom/Harvest/Planting   Bloom/Harvest/Planting

Maintenance   Maintenance

Planning   Planning

DECEMBER

WEEK 3   year_____

Weather

Bloom/Harvest/Planting

Maintenance

Planning

year_____   year_____

Weather

Weather

Bloom/Harvest/Planting

Bloom/Harvest/Planting

Maintenance

Maintenance

Planning

Planning

DECEMBER

WEEK 4   year_____

Weather

Bloom/Harvest/Planting

Maintenance

Planning

year_____   year_____

Weather   Weather

Bloom/Harvest/Planting   Bloom/Harvest/Planting

Maintenance   Maintenance

Planning   Planning

year_____

year_____

year_____

Summary

Summary

Summary

RESOURCES